EPILEPSY

If You Can't Do It Right, Just Do It Properly

Written by Gavin Hogarth

AuthorHouse™ UK
1663 Liberty Drive
Bloomington, IN 47403 USA
www.authorhouse.co.uk
Phone: 0800.197.4150

Published by AuthorHouse   11/24/2017

ISBN: 978-1-5462-8049-1 (sc)
ISBN: 978-1-5462-8048-4 (e)

authorHOUSE®

CHAPTER 1

THE BEGINNING

WHEN I WAS FIFTEEN YEARS old, I developed epilepsy. I had gone to work with my older brother delivering tyres for a company. My brother said to me, "Go and get me these types of tyres please." So I walked over to the van. As I started to walk back with the tyres on my arms, my brother said to me, "They are the wrong type." But by then I was no more aware than a zombie and just collapsed to the floor.

I was taken to the hospital, where I was diagnosed with epilepsy. My brother, having heard this from the doctor, got on the phone to ring our mum and told her what had happened. She thought it was a joke and said, "No one in our family has ever suffered from this problem."

"Well," my brother said, "he does now."

He then drove all the way from Blackpool down to Liverpool to pick up my mum.

When they got to the hospital, my mum listened to what the doctor had to say and then came to see how I was feeling. I was told that I was able to go home that night since I had no serious problems or injuries, and all three of us drove home to Liverpool. This was fine with me because I slept all the way from the hospital to our house.

I stayed in the house for a good couple of days and slowly started to get my self-confidence back. I then, bit by bit, began to go out a little.

One day, I was going to town to do some shopping. All of a sudden, I didn't have a clue where I was. I thought about this for a couple of minutes and then decided to call a close friend on my mobile phone. I told him what had happened. He asked, "Is there anything that you can see that might tell me where you are?" I didn't recognise anything at all. So my friend suggested I walk down to the driver and ask him what bus I was on. Would you believe I was on the wrong bus to start with?

My friend then said, "Get off the bus, and I will come and pick you up and help you home," which he did. When we got home, I thanked him for everything that he had done for me and then went straight upstairs to bed.

By this time, I was being treated at the Walton Hospital, and oh my; I must be the luckiest person in the history of the world (ever). You see, I was not being treated by any old doctor. Oh no, I was being treated by the professor of neurology and neurosurgery, a clinical specialist in epilepsy, who had a world-class reputation.

At this time, I was only having small fits (petit mal), where I was fully conscious. But I could still really feel the pain of falling down. I was just getting off the bus over the road from my house and had another small fit. I fell off the bus and into the road. You can just imagine what it feels like to see that you are covered in blood and painting the floor with it. A very nice, concerned lady came over and asked me where I lived. I pointed vaguely across the road and told the lady my name. The bus driver had already called an ambulance when the lady walked over to my house. When my mum opened the door, the lady said, "Does your son suffer from epilepsy?"

My mum said, "Oh no. What has he done now? Where is he?"

The lady pointed over the road to the bus stop, by which time the ambulance had turned up.

The paramedics were tending my wounds and trying to get my blood pressure under control, and then my mum and I were off to hospital. When we arrived, I was rushed into the X-ray department, and a short time later, I was told that I had a broken nose. Doctors said they would have to break it again to get it back into place.

This produced an unexpected effect: I have no sense of smell whatsoever, which has caused further repercussions. There was a time when my mum was not feeling too well and I said I would cook dinner. (An epileptic using a frying pan?) I served up in the dining room, and we started eating. The other problem was that my mum has no sense of smell either. (We made a great pair living together and trying to look after each other.) Well, a couple of minutes after we started, my sister arrived home and sat down next to us. At this point, we were all talking away, and then my sister said that there was a strong smell of burning. I got up and walked into the kitchen to see what it was. Now, would you believe the whole of one kitchen wall was on fire because I had left the frying pan on the stove? We had to call out the fire brigade.

It was not long after this incident that I started to have both the small fits (*petit mal*) but also seizures of the grand mal variety. I found out that I actually preferred to have these new ones, for the simple reason that I didn't feel any pain—because I was completely unconscious. The only way I knew that something had happened to me was when I woke up covered in blood. And I would have a terrible headache that lasted for hours.

A few days later, I got a letter from the hospital, so my mum and I went to see the professor, who asked me how I was doing. Now, I am always under the impression that honesty is the best policy, especially when your health is concerned. So I told him about my new fits, and he asked just how often I was having them. When he'd heard all the details, he said that a new drug was being tested and coming out, and it just might be able to help me. He also explained what the side effects of this drug might include, such as anger and depression.

This was very prophetic. My mum and I went to Sainsbury's one day, and after we had finished there, we decided to go and have something to eat and drink in the café. Well, when we had finished and were on our way out, a security guard walked up to us and kicked my mum in the ankle. (I should explain that my mum suffers from post-polio and polio syndrome and her movements are painful at the best of times). When I saw this, I started a fight with the man. I was giving as good as I got, but then, suddenly, I found myself fighting four men, all of them twice the size of me. After a while, they picked me up and started to frog-march me out of the shop.

At about this time, the police turned up at the car park and came over to me. When they heard what had happened, an officer said, "Just sit down for a minute and try and take it easy."

My mum then told them about my medication being changed, and the officer said, "All right then. It's okay for you to go home."

When we got home, my mum said, "Why did that just happen?"

I told her straight back, "As soon as I saw that man kick you, I just lost control and wanted to hurt him back."

CHAPTER 2

INTERNATIONAL FITS

WE HAD DECIDED THAT WE needed to go on a holiday to try to relax. We had to get to the airport at five o'clock in the morning, as we were expected to check in at quarter to six. When we landed, we were going to spend time with our family and friends, do all the parks, and go to a place called Water World, which had some big water slides. We were also going to spend a day at the NASA Space Center.

Well, as you might imagine, this was the best day ever for me. I cannot even begin to guess how much money I spent that day. Astronaut food and cans of soup! The day after, we all went to a place called Gatorland. This place was also really great, although one thing you don't want to do is to lean out over the barriers!

The next day, my mum and I, along with our friends, were walking around on the beach. The weather was perfect for sunbathing and we were having a great time, but our friends thought it was quite cold for Florida, so the next day we started going around the shopping centres. At that time of the year, most of the stores had sales, with 50 per cent to 75 per cent off normal prices.

We got back home and started to get the dinner ready, and then I had a grand mal fit. First I fell backwards and bounced off the worktop, and then I fell forward onto my face. This caused injuries to both the back and front of my head, so I was like a zombie again, which does happen afterwards. And I was suffering from concussion.

The next day, we were out shopping and stopped for some lunch at McDonald's. At this point, I had no idea what was going on, including who was talking to me. Someone asked me, "What do you feel like?" But to be honest, I could not understand what was being said. I was looking up at the signs, but I couldn't read or understand anything around me.

When we got home that night, my mum realised the severity of the situation, so she called the professor and told him what had happened. She asked him for advice, and he said, "I have to stress that you do not ring for an ambulance, as you will be charged for the ambulance like you cannot imagine, and you would also be charged for any treatment and any medication that they might give you." Now, I don't know how all this sounds to everyone else in the universe, but to me it sounds really bloody expensive. The professor then said, "I suggest the best way to deal with the situation is to go tomorrow morning to the airport and I will ring ahead and organise an emergency flight home, and then get you to the hospital as soon as possible. I will get in touch with the airport at your end, tell them who I am, and stress what your medical needs are."

When we landed at Manchester airport, there was an ambulance waiting for us. No waiting at passport control either, oh no: our bags were ready for us, and then it was straight out and into the ambulance and on our way, complete with the lights and siren.

When we got to the hospital, the professor was outside waiting for us. Then they rushed me in for a brain scan to see if there were any other problems. I was then sent down to his ward, where we waited only a couple of minutes before he came back and said, "Well, it is my assessment from the scan results that you are suffering from something called epileptic-induced amnesia." He was unable to say just how long it would last, but it was a few weeks before I was able to leave the hospital. Finally, when I was able to go home, my mum, who had been a regular visitor at my bedside, came to me and said, "Well, here we go. We're going home, so let's get you dressed and then we can make a move."

Just as we were about to leave, the professor walked over to us from the other side of his ward and said to us both, "Remember now, just try to relax and keep calm, and whatever you do, don't let this get you down. At the end of the day, it's not your fault, okay? It's just something that we all need to just push through, so all the best now, mate, and we will see you soon all right?"

Then my mum said, "Thanks for everything you have done for us." Then she shook his hand, and said to me, "Say thank you, now," which I did, and then we walked outside and got a taxi home.

I still have trouble remembering certain facts, such as people's names, and it takes me ages before I get to know something properly. At least, though, I don't suffer from amnesia anymore, although retaining information can still be an issue.

There was another incident soon afterwards, when we went on another holiday. The amnesia had started to clear up, so I was getting many of my memories back, and once again I was on a new medication. But we had not been on the plane for long before another issue arose. There was a family sitting behind us (the mum and dad and a little boy and girl). The girl was right behind my seat, and she must have thought that kicking the chair in front of her as hard and as fast as she could possibly do would help pass the time. After a while, I got up and turned around and politely asked both the parents, "Could you please ask your daughter to stop kicking the back of my seat?" But a couple of minutes later, wouldn't you know it, she was at it again, kicking harder and faster than before. I tolerated this for a little bit, but then something snapped, and I turned around and grabbed a puzzle book that she was holding and smacked her on the top of her head.

We were quickly moved to the back of the plane, and then the plane started to turn around and head back to the airport. When we had landed I was met by multiple police officers, all armed with both MP5s and pistols. They placed a pair of handcuffs on me and then walked me into a room. One said, "Stand up against the wall and don't move." There were two guards in the room with my mum and me; the rest of them had gone into the family room for a talk with them about the situation.

However, just before they walked out, my mum rang the family solicitor, who said, "It's okay. I am in the area and will be right down. I will only be a couple of minutes. See you soon." When she arrived she told the guards that I should not have been handcuffed behind my back. She then said, "I would like you to take the handcuffs off and let him sit down, okay?" I was led into the cells and placed in a single cell for the night; meanwhile, our solicitor spoke to the family to try to find a way that we could work the situation out.

The family said that they didn't want to press any charges against me—just because they just wanted to go on their holiday. With this, our solicitor walked in to see my mum and said to her, "It's okay. No charges are going to be pressed. However, they will be keeping him in overnight. But don't worry. The airport hotel will give you a room for the night, and then you both can go home."

My mum said, "Thank you very much for your help," and they shook hands.

When I was placed in the cell I lay down on the bed. I must admit that it didn't take me long to realise that it was, at the end of the day, all my own fault that I was here in the first place. All of a sudden, a guard opened the hole in the cell door and said, "Full name?" This must have happened every hour; just as you were managing to get back to sleep, the hole would open again for you to reply to the same question. In the morning, the door opened and the guard said, "Come on, it's time to go."

He walked me out, and I saw the look on my mum's face and I thought, *Oh no*, and then my mum said, "You're very lucky that the family didn't want to press any charges." Well, you could say that this was the second time that I had been in trouble with the police, although I still didn't have any formal record with them.

CHAPTER 3

WOULD YOU TRUST ME DRIVING AROUND?

IT DIDN'T TAKE LONG FOR me to learn from the professor that there was no chance I would ever hold a driving licence. I must admit I was planning to apply, but after he told me this story, I could see why I would not.

"Imagine that you're driving around and turn off into a street, and then, all of a sudden—BANG!—you have trouble with your epilepsy and lose control of the car and drive into the gates of a junior school and either injure or kill some kids and their parents. Is there any way you could forgive yourself for that? Okay, it might not be your fault, but it is exactly for reasons like this that we must put our foot down and say no. You see, everyone in the world has the right to be given the chance to live, wouldn't you agree?"

Well, I did think about this for a couple of seconds, and I decided that he did have a very good point. There was no way I would ever be able to forgive myself if I was in a situation like that, so I said, "Yes, I see what you mean, and I promise you that I will never try to get a licence—not that they would give me one." So there was no chance of me ever having a driving licence in my lifetime. But then I thought, so what? You should just put it out of your mind and stop thinking, *How could this happen to me?* And it was then that I thought, *Well, if you can think of your life with your epilepsy and never let it get you down, then you are never going to get depressed about any of your injuries.*

So I decided to do this: every time I had an accident or found myself covered in plaster, I would do is look in the mirror and just have the best laugh at myself. Just tell myself, *Oh yes! You have really done it now!* And I'd let that pick up my self-confidence. And believe me, it is definitely the best way to make sure that you can beat the sadness. To say to yourself, *It's just another day at the office,* and just enjoy your life no matter what. It could be just as bad tomorrow or the next day, but so what?

Now I will tell you some of the other things that have happened to me over the years. And if you cannot have a good laugh with me at my life, then you have not understood epilepsy to begin with.

Here's a good one that involves a grand mal. I was walking into my bedroom and then, bang! I bounced off the radiator, and as I was bouncing off it, I hit my head on my bedroom door. I was then trapped behind my door, thrashing away against the back of the door and the radiator. While all this was happening, my little dog was barking like mad. You see, he was a rescue dog, and we were told that he had been terribly abused and neglected as a puppy (it took us a good couple of months before he realised that he was a part of our family and our friend). Anyway, after a while, every time I had a fit, he would run over to my mum and start to bark and jump up and down, and it was then that

Mum would realise that something was wrong. Having got her attention, my dog would then run out of the room and lead her to where I was. We didn't train this dog to do this. I think it the dog was simply pleased that he was part of a lovely family and thought he should help.

After I had this fit, I woke up on the floor of my bedroom and then walked downstairs to get a good cup of coffee. This happened on a Friday night, and I was going around like normal with no apparent problems, and when my carer came to our house to pick me up to go out together for the day, I said to him, "Will you do me a favour please and just have a look at this ankle?" It had started to swell up, and I don't mean just mild swelling; it had also gone about four different colours. After seeing it, my carer said, "I think we should get you to the hospital to get it checked out, just to see what is going on, okay?" In the end I was in the hospital for only about an hour, and they then said I could go home.

CHAPTER 4

LET'S JUST HAVE A BREAK

I HAD A SMALL BREAK up the front of my left leg, and they had already placed the plaster on my leg before telling me that I could have had a choice of colours. Well, I was shocked to see that they had chosen a horribly bright and "pretty" pink.

A good while later, they took the plaster off and told me I could go home. It was just coming up to New Year's Eve, and I had taken some drinks up for my mum, and then I turned around and was going down the stairs to get two cans of Guinness for myself. What do you think happened next? I had a small fit and fell down the stairs, bouncing around as I went. I was told by the ambulance service that they were sure my leg was broken. So we got to the hospital, and I was taken into the X-ray department, where they confirmed that it was in almost the same place but this time the other leg. So within a couple of months I had now broken both legs, but because it had not been too long since my plaster had come off my other leg, they didn't think it would be wise to let me walk on it, so I was given a wheelchair to help me get around.

However, there was one problem—I live on a bit of a hill. It was okay to go *down* the hill, although I had to keep control of my speed as much as possible, and this alone took some time, but the hardest thing was trying to get back up to the house, and that was even harder with the shopping. I have nothing but the highest respect for all disabled people, no matter the nature of their disability, but the last thing an epileptic needs is to have a fit while trying to get up a hill. Anyway, I was going up to my home with the shopping in my lap and the handles of the food bags in my mouth, pushing like mad, and it must have taken me at least ten minutes to get to my house, but I didn't let it get me down.

Two months before I went back to the hospital and they took off the plaster from my legs. The doctor then said to me, "Can you get up on both legs and try to walk around the room for me please." As I tried to do this, I found out quite quickly that both my legs were giving away at times. After watching me, the doctor said, "How about a pair of crutches?" I took them off him and tried to walk around, but I could not do it. I would be just starting to walk around when all of a sudden my legs would give way again. I fell forward into his office door and hit my head on the way down, and he agreed that crutches would not be the best thing to give an epileptic, because if I fell forward, I would not be able to put my hands out to save myself. This could cause me more harm, but because we had come with a wheelchair, the doctor said that I could go home, but I shouldn't put too much pressure on my legs, as this would just cause me more pain, and it would take my legs longer than normal to heal.

So we got home and I was very weak, but I could just about manage to get around. I was not going to let this one beat me, but I must admit that I was spending a lot of my time in my bed just resting. (In so doing, I was also very close to the toilet; you don't want to have to go up the stairs to get to the toilet, so it was best that I stayed close by.)

We went back to the hospital a couple of weeks later and the doctor asked me, "How are you feeling?" I said that there was no more pain, and I was able to use both legs again. They then sent me down to the X-ray department and looked at both my legs, and then they sent us down to his office.

He was sitting at his desk, looking at the X-ray pictures on his computer screen. My mum and I both sat down, and then he turned around to face us both and said, "I have some news for you. The breaks to both your legs have managed to repair themselves. But just remember that if you have a fall and land on either leg, this could easily happen again, and it would be twice as bad and twice as painful. It would also make the first injuries much worse, so just try to be careful with yourself." I must admit, I don't really think that this really applies to someone who has epilepsy.

Not long after this happened, I was sneaking out the back door of my house (because the front door was locked; when the dogs hear anything around the back door, they automatically start barking, thinking that someone is breaking into the house). I was going out one night to go over the road to get myself a pack of cigarettes, and I had just got to the door when I had a grand mal fit. When I woke up, I was lying on the floor, very much like a zombie, just lying in my pyjamas and a T-shirt. It was very windy that night, and the rain was very heavy, so I got up onto my feet and then walked back into the house and went to bed. I had a couple of hours' sleep, and then I got up to go to the toilet, and it was then that I noticed my cap was not where it was supposed to be.

For some reason, I decided to go down and try to find it, so I went down and opened the door and found my jeans, my jumper, and my cap just lying around dripping wet and very cold. I picked them both up, brought them into the kitchen, and put them on the floor by the washing machine and went back to bed. When I woke up in the morning, I noticed in the bathroom mirror that there was blood all down face, and when I started to get dressed I noticed that there was blood dripping from my bedclothes. So I called my mum, and she popped her head up the stairs and said, "Are you all right there?"

I shouted back, "Can you please help me?"

She came up to my bedroom and saw the state of me and said, "Just wait a minute and I will go and get the first aid kit." When she came back, she started to wipe the blood off my face, and then she then noticed that there was a small amount of blood dripping down from my mouth. "Open your mouth and show me your tongue," she said. You see, I have both an over- and an under-bite, and I had bitten into the top and bottom of the left side of my tongue.

I rang my dentist and asked for an emergency appointment, and the lady said, "Can you get here in the next five minutes?"

I replied, "Yes, I only live around the corner."

We got to the dentist, and the dentist said, "Lie down and show me your tongue," and he had a good look at it. "I do see the damage to your tongue; however, I am very sorry, but there is nothing that I can do for you, as I can't give you any medication for it, and I cannot stitch it back together for you. I think there is only one way that this injury will repair, and that's to stop eating any hard or sticky foods. The only thing I can recommend is to let it get better in its own time. All you are going to be able to eat is soup, and even then it will take a while before it gets better. However, the scar will be there forever."

"Thank you very much for your time," I said, and we shook hands. Then Mum and I went home. It must a good few weeks before I was able to start to eat properly and have decent food and drinks, but when that finally happened, I felt as though I was having the time of my life.

The best way that I have found of handling epilepsy is never to let it get you down, as this will only lead to depression. And believe me, I have been there and gotten the T-shirt. You don't need that in your life, so the best way to get on and handle your epilepsy is to just pick yourself up after each fit, have a good look at yourself in the mirror, and have a really good laugh at yourself. Tell yourself that, *Yes, this one is definitely better than the previous one.* It also helps to take a picture of each and every injury you get, as this will show any people who work for the disability benefits or any other departments the extent of the challenges you face. Above all, just remember to keep your hopes up at all times.

CHAPTER 5

THE POOL INCIDENT

NEXT I WAS TOLD BY the good professor, "If you start regular swimming, it might help you with the epilepsy a little bit." So that is what I did with my mum every week. While we were there, we met up with a man called Ken, and we would have a good chat, and after a while we got to know each other very well. Ken was a teacher from a local school. One week later, Ken was talking to my mum, and I was just swimming around the pool, and what do you think happened next? I had a grand mal fit while in the pool, and I slowly started to sink. Ken placed his arms around me and pulled me to the surface of the water.

There was a lifeguard on duty, but he was just sitting there reading the newspaper, and he didn't even notice what was happening to me. However, there was another lifeguard on duty as well. She was a very little woman, but when she noticed what had happened to me, she jumped into the water and started to get me out of the pool with my mum and our new friend, Ken. It took four people to get me out. I was taken into the men's changing room and placed into a special space blanket to keep me warm. When I woke up, I didn't recognise anybody, but then I smiled as I started to remember some of the people around me. Once I got dressed and started to wake up properly, I managed to get home with my mum's help, and then I got changed and got into bed.

In the morning, I had a really bad headache, which was always at the back of my head. This always happens for hours at a time and is very painful. You don't want to do anything that day except sit still—but where is the fun in doing that? It is like putting yourself down, and if you do this to yourself, just imagine what you could be missing out on. Like getting on with your day and working through it, it's best to try to not to think about your headache and just work your way through it and try to enjoy life as best you can.

Now, when my professor heard about this, I was asked, "Do you mind if I switch your medication around a little?" I mean, what could I say? "No, you can't"? I don't think so, so I said, "I'm more than willing to give it a go." I don't mind trying anything out that might help, and also there were a good few medical students sitting in the room, with white coats and notepads.

Before the professor and I had started talking, he said to the students, "Remember now, you cannot talk to each other or to either of us, so just keep taking your notes. I hope that this is understood, all right?" So the medical students never made a sound; all they did was listen to us and write on their pads. I thought this could be helpful in the long run, because at the end of the day, you never know who will be taking over from either the professor himself or someone under him.

The professor was not pleased that my new medication was not working as well as he had hoped. You see, I had recently managed to break my all-time record for a number of fits that I had sustained in one day, which now stood at forty-two, and I had sustained many injuries. However, I didn't cause myself any harm every time, as most of the time I was in bed during my fits. Now, about three months later, I had started to have a great many more grand mal fits—four in one day—and was having the petit mal fits as well. So, naturally, I was having a great time, getting lots of injuries from landing on the floor on my face. I had lost a lot of blood, as you might imagine, so when an ambulance arrived at my house after a particularly bad incident, they placed me in the straps on the stretcher so I couldn't fall off it if I had another fit. They then decided to put a line in my arm to slow down the bleeding.

My mum and I were taken into hospital, and when we arrived at the A&E department and they treated my injuries, they decided that I should have a CT scan just to make sure there were no sign of lumps growing on my brain or any signs of bleeding. Well, I was lucky, as there was nothing whatsoever. They decided that I should spend time in the serious head trauma unit (SHTU), just to make sure that I was doing all right. While I was there I had two more grand mal fits, but luckily there were a good few people on the ward, and when I was having a fit and I woke them up, they would quickly press the emergency button to call for the staff. The bars were always up so that I couldn't fall out of the bed, and they decided that I should spend another two days in hospital. There were no more problems after the first day, so the doctor said to my mum, "I am very sorry to say this, but he seems fine now, and they need the beds." So Mum went straight up to the desk and signed the papers, and then the two of us were on our way home.

We got a taxi home and I went straight to bed, but the very next day I had another grand mal fit. When I woke up I didn't notice any difference, but then I went into the bathroom and glanced in the mirror—and I didn't know who or what was looking back at me.

CHAPTER 6

EYE EYE

Two of the biggest black eyes that I have ever seen in my life. Not only that, but in just another couple of days, I started to have more petit mal fits, and one day I managed to break my world record for petit mal fits in a day, which stood at forty-two. It had shot right the way up to stand at *sixty-eight* in a single day, and believe me, there were a good few injuries that day. Well, the next time that I had a fit, I was walking out of the kitchen when I collapsed to the floor. I got up and walked over to the back door to let the dogs in, then closed it behind me. I had to just sit down for a couple of seconds, afraid to stand up now.

After that I used my hands and knees; that way I wouldn't have so far to fall. I was sitting on the floor watching television, and I noticed that there was blood dripping down my face. On this particular day, just before this happened, my mum had gone out shopping with my sister, and it seemed like a lifetime while I waited for them to get back. When they did, the two of them started to bring the shopping into the house, and both the dogs started barking like mad. The living room door was closed, and they finished bringing the shopping out of the car into the house.

When it was all put away, my sister said, "Okay, Mum, I am going to make a move. I am in work in the morning, and it's been changed from 5 a.m. to 8 p.m." So while she was leaving and my mum was saying goodbye to her, Mum noticed that the dogs hadn't stopped barking yet. She opened the door, and there I was, lying on the floor, covered in blood again. My mum came over and said, "Oh, not again. What happened to you this time?" Then she said, "Sam has just left, but don't worry. I will get on the phone and ring for an ambulance," which she did. Now, you see, I am very lucky indeed, because my mum is an ex-nurse and my sister, Sam, is a nurse, and both my older brothers are fully trained first-aid officers as well.

When my mum was on the phone to the emergency services, I was having a great deal of petit mal fits, one after another, so the person on the other end asked my mum, "Is that your son having his fits?" My mum replied that it was. The lady on the phone then said, "Will you keep talking to him please—and please don't put the phone down. Can you also get to the front door and open it please." My mum walked out of the room and opened the front door and put the dogs out in the back garden so that the ambulance people could do their work on me. She then walked back in, and the lady on the phone said to her, "Could you please confirm each and every one of his fits for us, while we are on the phone. The ambulance will not be long. I guarantee you this, as I have marked it as urgent." We could now hear the ambulance, and we noticed the lights as well. I am sure that all my neighbours hated me as if I were hell itself, but they all know me now, and they understand what the score is.

The ambulance staff got the bleeding under control and then put in the IV drip. I said to them, "I bet you a fiver that you don't manage to get that needle in my arm in less than four goes."

The medic replied, "Now, don't you worry about anything. I am very good at this." When he got the lines in, he had to secure them with a bandage to keep them in place.

Now, I have a great respect for medics because I use their services so much; however, there are two things that I know really well: the first is epilepsy and the second is my body's reactions. Well, the medic could not get the first line in, so he tried for the second one in the same arm, and he couldn't get this one in either. He tried a third time in the other arm, and would you believe it, he could not get this one in either. In fact, he managed to get the IV in on the fourth attempt, just like I said.

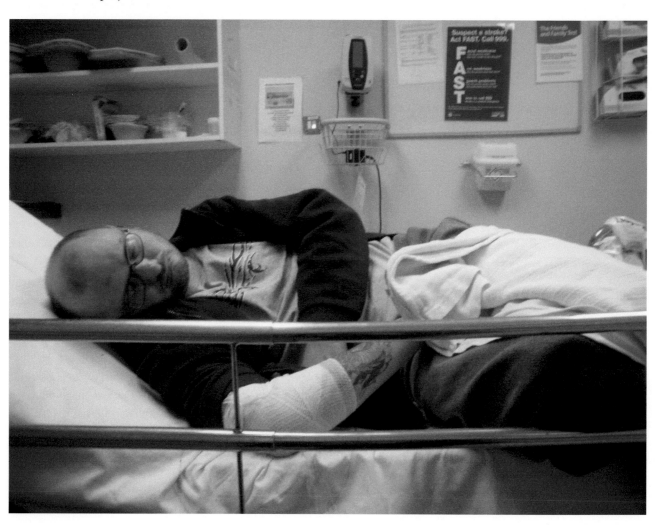

CHAPTER 7

THE HOSPITAL INCIDENT

ONCE THE MEDICS HAD GOT the IV into me, they gave me something to slow down the bleeding. Then I was asked the most stupid question for a person with epilepsy: "Can you describe your pain level for me please, 1 meaning not too bad and 10 meaning the worst."

Now, I would just like to say that I personally fucking hate getting asked this question. I mean, as someone who has a high pain level all the time because of falling down and receiving all these injuries, how can I answer this question in a nutshell? Anyway, when I was asked the question, I said to him, "I would say that it feels like a 3." Now, a 3 may seem low, eliciting a response like, "Oh just give him an aspirin." But my pain level 3 is someone else's 7. So you see, they cannot understand what you are trying to tell them, but every time you are in hospital, these are the first words out of someone's mouth, and as I said, this really pissed me off. So I was placed on the stretcher, and my mum and all the medics and I were on our way to hospital. Now, when I fell down in the kitchen, because of the amount of pain I was in at the time, I was convinced that my ankle was broken, so when we arrived at the hospital, I was taken into the trauma unit.

The place was packed with all kinds of people on stretchers and in wheelchairs, and for every person that was waiting to be seen to, there were also two drivers that could not leave the hospital until you had been taken into the trauma unit and had turned over your medical records to the staff. Naturally, the worst cases went in first and the less urgent were moved around and seen to at a different time. While I and my mum and the drivers were waiting, I said to my mum, "Will you please do me a favour and go back home and get your head down and let the dogs back in?"

She was pleased to hear me say this, and considering that it was almost two o'clock in the morning, she said, "Yes, all right then. I will see you soon. Take it easy now for me, okay?" I got out my mobile phone and give my friend Ken a call and told him what had happened and asked if he could come up. This friend of mine is the type of person who will do anything for anyone he knows.

He asked me if I was on my house phone, which is always right by my side. When Ken turns up, he always brings a camera with him to take pictures of my injuries. There is a very good reason for taking pictures of your injuries, namely, so you have something to show in disability or benefits interviews about yourself and your lifestyle. When I was taken into the trauma unit, I had bitten a good-sized piece of my top lip, and I was still having loads of small fits, so I was told by the nurse, "I cannot give you anything for the pain, so will you just have to try and think nice, happy thoughts."

I was lying down, and every time I had a fit or made a sound, she would stop and stand still and ask, "Are you okay?" Well, how the heck would I know that? I was told, "You are doing very well," and then, "Okay, there we go. It is all done." I was then sent straight down to the X-ray department to see just how much damage, if any, had been detected, and after that I was taken back to the trauma unit.

A doctor came up to me and said, "Hi, there. Well, we have looked at your X-ray, and you will be happy to hear that your ankle is not broken or fractured. It's just a case of severe swelling of the surrounding tissue. If you don't mind, we would like to admit you for a couple of days, just to see how you get on with it, okay?" Well, what are you going to say them? At the end of the day, they are doing you a favour by looking after your medical needs.

I was taken up to a ward and placed on a bed. Now don't get me wrong, but we were all very bored, mostly because there was nothing to do apart from having meals and drinks and snacks, or perhaps you can play on a mobile phone or computer that a family member or friend has brought in.

One time, my mum rang the hospital and gave them my full name, date of birth, and address and asked how I was, but the person on the phone said to her, "I hope you realise that I cannot give you that kind of information. Your son is a thirty-nine-year-old man, and if he wanted you to know, I am sure that he would have rung you up and let you know, so I am very sorry." She then put the phone down on my mum. I suppose you can see it from the hospital's point of view; however, my mum was not a bit pleased.

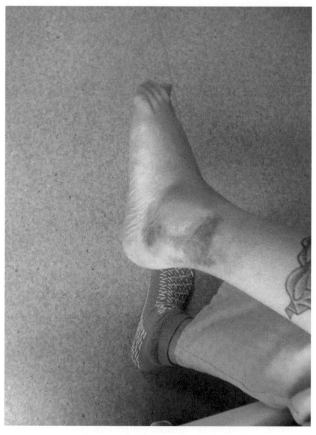

One time a stupid student doctor suddenly put his head around the curtain and walked in to see me. He then started laughing at a very high volume. To be honest, I didn't think the most of him from the first time we met, but at the end of the day, it's each to their own, is it not? He then sat down on the corner of the bed with a notepad in his hands, and the first question that I got from him was, "Well, then, what is the best way that you can describe your experience with your epilepsy?" I mean, how are you supposed to answer a question like that? "I fall down a lot and fall into things from time to time, and I've fallen down the stairs a couple of times"? Or should I have mentioned all the other things that had happened over the years?

So I said to him, "Well, what do you want me to say? Both of us know about epilepsy, although I bet I know a little bit more about it than you do."

He replied, "Ho now, let's not be like this with each other."

I thought about this for a couple of seconds and replied, "All right then, but I bet I know the next questions you want to ask me."

He looked at me as if I were stupid and said, "All right, let's just see how good you are."

I looked up at him and said, "Okay. I should think, then, that there are a fair amount of questions you could ask me, are there not?"

He looked down at his notepad, which he had not even opened yet, then looked up at me and said, "Let's see if you can name at least two of the questions I have on my note pad, okay?"

I replied, "Okay then, let's see now … What you want to know is just how many fits I have a week, and also per month, and per year. Am I right?"

He said, "Yes you are, and could you answer those questions for me please."

I looked at him and said, "Well, the answer is *no*, I cannot tell you how often I have fits, and that is because my epilepsy is uncontrollable, so I don't get any warning signs—no funny smells or anything else. You see, one minute I might be sitting down or walking around, and then bang, straight down to the floor. And then sometimes it is back to hospital, although we have three fully useable first aid kits around my house and my mum often sees to my injuries; this way we can cut down on a number of times that we have to ring for an ambulance. So what do you think about all that then, mate? There must have been at least five or six questions. So what do you say? Am I right or did I fail?"

The young student looked up at me and said, "Yes, you are right about all the questions I was told to ask you. In total, there are fifteen questions they ask you on a regular basis just to make sure you are not changing your answers, and I must say that I am very sorry, because out of fifteen, you got eleven right straight away, and this is a great score. I would just like to say that we both know about epilepsy, but because you live with it, you do know more than I ever will."

I then replied, "Don't ever put yourself down, and never disrespect anyone else or judge them for what they might be going through, all right?"

"Yes, and thank you so very much. This has been a total eye-opener for me, and I think it will stand me in good stead for a good few years." He got up and reached out for my hand and said, "Thanks again for everything." Then he walked out of the ward, and I never saw him again.

For the whole time I was on the ward, five days in total, I could walk around to the bathroom and the shower. Then, on the fifth day, a nurse came to see me and said, "I have some news for you. You are being discharged from hospital today. We are just waiting for your mum to come and pick you up, okay?"

"Yes, fine thanks," I replied.

I started to get dressed and to pack up all my stuff. I had just sat down on my bed after coming back from the toilet, when all of a sudden this very good-looking woman walked over to me and sat down on the corner of my bed.

"Why, hello there. Would you mind if I asked you a question?"

"Please go ahead," I replied, and with that, I got the biggest story of crap that I have ever heard in my life, which was even more shocking because it was coming from a lady's mouth.

She looked at me and said, "Do you believe in God?"

I thought, *Oh no, not another one of these questions*, and I replied, "Yes, I do believe in God, why?"

"So then you do believe that God is all-knowing and forgives all?"

"Yes, I believe in God, too. However, I think my point of view is a bit different from that of others."

Then I heard one of the stupidest questions in my life. "Well, do you not believe that God himself could come down from heaven and cure your illness?"

"Well, go on then. Please explain to me how he is going to do all of this for me."

Then came a story that was the biggest load of crap from start to finish. "Well, what God will do for you is come down from heaven and go up to a doctor in the corridor and place his hands on his head, and then the doctor will be able to walk over to you and, by touching you, cure all your health problems."

Now, I must say that I apologise to anybody who believes in God, or whatever version of God they pray to—we are all praying to God, so does it matter which language we use? I don't care who believes in what, because at the end of the day it's each to their own, is it not? As I was saying, as soon as she had finished the session, which I was compelled to listen to, I just started laughing like mad at this woman, my tears falling like a great river and streaming down both sides of my face.

As you might imagine, I was having the greatest experience that I had ever had in my life to that day, but I think it might have upset her very deeply, as while I was laughing at her she got to her feet and in a loud voice said, "Whatever."

She was just about to walk over to another person on my ward when she noticed that everyone else on the ward was also laughing at her. She stormed out of the ward. Now, I must admit, this made me feel a little bit pissed off as well, so I got up off the bed and walked out into the corridor and said to the staff nurse, "Hiya, mate. Who the heck is that woman who is walking around and telling people about the power of God and that he will come down from heaven and touch a doctor and then they will cure me?"

He laughed and replied, "Are you serious about this?"

"Yes, I am."

"Can you describe her for me please?"

I was wondering how to explain what she looked like, but then, would you believe it, she came out of another ward and started walking down the corridor. I said, "That is her, there."

The staff nurse said, "Oh, not again. She should not even be able to gain access to the wards."

The lady did have an identity card hanging around her neck, but she was quickly and quietly escorted out of the hospital, after her identity card was taken off her.

CHAPTER 8

GETTING HOME FROM HOSPITAL?

WHEN WE LEFT THE HOSPITAL we naturally went straight home, and I was really ready for a big dinner, as I was starving after five days of hospital food. I sat down and ate, and then I went upstairs to get into my own bed. When I got up in the morning I had a couple of pieces of toast, and then, later on, when we were sat down for our dinner, the phone rang and I picked it up.

"Hello," said the person on the other end. "Is this Mr Gavin Hogarth?"

"Yes, speaking, can I help you?"

"Hello, I am a doctor from the hospital, and I was hoping that you might be able to come back into the hospital. I have just checked over your X-ray, and there is a small chance that it is fractured. Would you be able to get up here as soon as possible please?"

Well, I had just started my dinner and I had only been out of hospital for two days, so I said to him, "Can I just finished my dinner please?"

"Yes, I don't have a problem with that. I will leave your name behind the desk at the A&E department, so you will be able to go straight in to be checked out."

After the two of us had finished our dinner, we started the trip to the hospital. We walked into the A&E department and waited until it was our turn. After a while, I asked the lady behind the desk about being called in to be seen, but the lady had never heard of me. "I am sorry, but we have no idea what you are talking about. There is nothing here that says you are due to be seen to straightaway, so I need you to go into that department and wait for your name to be called. Thank you." So we went in and sat down, and there must have been at least seventy-five people there.

We sat there talking to each other for ages, when suddenly my name was called, so we walked into the doctor's room and told him what we had been told.

"Oh, I can see what the doctor meant. Does it hurt when I touch you here?"

"Yes, it does," I replied.

The doctor then touched a different place on my ankle. "Does this hurt when I touch it as well?"

Once again I replied, "Yes, it does."

He then had another look and feel around and said, "Okay, I'm sending you down to the fracture clinic. That leg is going to have to be put in plaster. Wait just a minute and I will call someone to come and take you down."

A few seconds later a lovely lady came in with a wheelchair and said, "Okay, going to take you down." We started our journey to the fracture clinic, and I was placed in a cubicle with a curtain around it. Once again I was waiting around for hours, so I said to one of the nurses, "Is there any chance you could tell me what time I might be seen to, as there is people who came in after I arrived being seen to first?"

The nurse said to me, "I am very sorry, but there are a lot of people in the world, and a good many of them are coming in here. Some of them might be a little bit more urgent than you are, okay?"

Well, what can you say to that? We waited around for our turn, and then a woman came into my room and said, "I am going to put your plaster on now. I will start at the back of your foot and then move up your leg. After I have done your ankle, I want you to push your foot as hard as you can, okay?"

"I will try my best for you, love," I said. "It's been a fair time since I saw a lady who is as good looking as yourself."

She replied, "I can see that you are a right charger, are you not? I don't even get spoken to by my husband like that anymore!"

I could not resist saying, "Oh no, this should be considered a national crime!"

"Okay then, that's it. You are all done. But don't forget that this is a non-weight-bearing plaster, all right?" She then asked my mum, "Will you be able to get him through the doors?"

"Oh yes, I will manage," she said. However, since my mum is on crutches as well, it was not going to be easy for her.

The nurse said to us, "Do you have your return date?"

"No," I said, "we were never told about that."

She went back onto the ward and brought an information sheet to us. "Here you go. All you have to do is ring a day in advance, all right?" We thanked her for all she had done for us. She waved to us both and then walked back into the ward. We then had to wait an hour and a half for a taxi to come and pick us up and take us home, and as you might imagine, my mum was *not* pleased with the level of service that we had been receiving.

It was after all of this happened that my mum decided to ring up the hospital's complaints department.

CHAPTER 9

THE COMPLAINT?

IN A ONE-IN-A-MILLION CHANCE, THE person who answered the phone was the chief complaints officer himself, so my mum started telling him about everything we had suffered and all the anxiety we'd experienced being given such a poor level of hospital service, and not just from one department but one after another. He replied, "I am very sorry to hear about this. Would you mind if I started to look into this account of your son's treatment here at the hospital?"

My mum said, "Yes, by all means, go ahead and see for yourself."

My mum told him my full name, date of birth, address, postcode, and phone number, and then she said to him, "Now, I want you to know that I am not going to stand down from this complaint whatsoever. Do you understand what it is that I am saying?"

"Yes, I do. We are committed to providing the very best treatment for each and every patient, and we not stand for anything that doesn't make that standard. I really would like you to appreciate this."

My mum thanked him for everything that he had said.

About two weeks later we were due to go back into the fracture clinic to see about my leg, so my mum rang up. The only reason that she rings people for me is that I have the memory of a very small goldfish who is just swimming around in its very little world, whereas she can remember things and describe them to other people for me. We rang the fracture clinic and asked them what time my appointment was. Well, the lady on the phone said, "Who? I am very sorry to say this, but I don't have any times for anyone with that name."

Once again, my mum was *not* pleased. She replied, "Oh don't worry about it. You see, I have a complaint with the chief complaints officer, so I will just ring him and find out from him, after mentioning the little talk we have just had. Thank you very much."

The lady on the end of the phone must have had a massive shock, as straightaway she said, "Oh, I have just noticed that we do have an appointment for two o'clock this afternoon, if this would be all right with you."

My mum was smiling at me as she said, "Okay, then. We will be down for that time. Thank you."

We got down to the hospital and had just sat down when my name was called. We walked into a room, I lay down, and the lady cut off the plaster. Once it was off, a doctor walked in and looked at it, and I said, "Does this mean you are going to be taking another X-ray of my ankle and my foot?"

The doctor replied, "Oh no, we will just use your first one; however, I can see from just looking at it that you now need to have a boot placed on your leg. This will have to remain on for at least two weeks. The nurse will bring one down for you and show you how to use it, okay? Thanks again and goodbye."

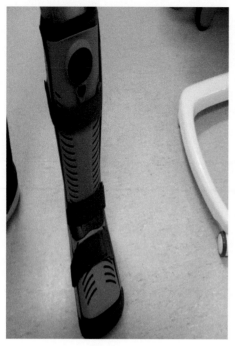

With that he just walked out. The nurse showed me how to put it on and take it off. I had it on and was walking around with it and people were looking at me, and I thought, *Well, if they cannot understand my situation, then that is their problem, not mine.* I don't give a shit about what anyone else thinks, and I don't mind walking around with strange things on my body. This is my world, not yours.

So I went to my local pub to have a few drinks and a few games of pool with my carers. As you might imagine, I do know quite a few people from the pub, since someone who has epilepsy does get noticed very quickly. None of them care about my condition. I can just walk in and start saying hello to everyone I know, and I am very pleased about this. However, this time, the landlord came out from the back, looked at my foot, and said, "What the hell happened to you this time?" I told him about the incident, and he started laughing at me like mad. "Oh, I am very sorry, I didn't mean—"

I jumped in, "Oh, yes you did, but don't worry about me. I don't give a shit about what happens. All I do is just pick myself back up and get on with my life."

He said, "I am amazed that you can see it that way."

I replied, "Well, if I didn't I would go mad, so I just enjoy my life. At the end of the day it's just another day at the office."

After a while it was time to get the boot removed from my foot, and both the doctor and the nurse had a very good look at the bruising. The doctor said, "It's still got a good deal of bruising all around both of your ankles, so try not to put too much pressure on it, all right?"

I replied, "And how am I going to do that, considering that I live in a house with three bedrooms and two living rooms?"

The doctor said, "Well, could you not move your bedroom downstairs?"

"Well, yes, I think that I could do that."

"Well, that's what I think is the best thing for you to do."

I was having a good laugh in my mind as I replied to this, "Oh yes, that is a very good idea, but just how am I supposed to get upstairs to get to the bathroom and to use the toilet?"

"Oh, I didn't know that your toilet was upstairs."

I came straight back at him and said, "Yes, and that's why I have now broken the same ankle twice so far. I am not sure if you can imagine what I am talking about, but believe me, the pain level gets enormously worse each time I have these injuries." Then I said, "So what do you think is best? Should I just lie down on the floor or pick myself up and then get on with my life? Personally, I have always gone for the getting up off your arse and getting on with your life. Don't you think that's best?"

As you can imagine, the doctor responded, "Yes, I do think that your way of living with it is the best way for you."

A short time later, my mum rang the complaints department again to see what was being done about my case.

CHAPTER 10

AFTER BOOT CAMP

WELL, SOON AFTER, THE TWO doctors and the nurse walked out into the corridor and started talking to each other, and a short time later, all of them walked back into the room and the head doctor said, "Mr Hogarth, we have noticed that there is another problem with your foot. You see, the problem was just treated was a swollen ankle to begin with, and then, after a week, it was upgraded to a fracture, and then, after the plaster was taken off a boot was put on—and because we didn't notice the break—I am sorry to say that you will have to be called in for a operation, and we will have to place metal screws in your ankle. I do believe that we should get you upstairs and prepared for surgery as soon as possible."

I thought about this and concluded that it needed to be done, so I might as well get it over with. I replied to the doctor, "Well, it seems that there is nothing else to be done is there, so let's get on with it."

"Okay, we will take you upstairs and you will be the first patient on the list for surgery. When the operation is over, you will wake up in the post-op room, and you will be feeling very uneasy about what happened to you, but it will soon pass. All right then, here we go. See you soon."

When we arrived in the operating theatre, it didn't seem to take too long for me to go right off to sleep, which is not normal for me; I think the anaesthetic could have been a contributing factor. It was a big bang when I started to wake up. It only seemed like a couple of minutes to me, although in fact, I was in the operating room for just over three and a half hours. They kept me in the hospital for two weeks after the operation, during which time I learned how to start walking around again. I was told not to try too hard. "Just start slowly and then build it up a little bit more over time," they said.

As you can imagine, it took a very long time to get better. The more it hurt, the more I would make myself go through the exercises. It did not take long for them to come and look over my leg and my ankle. They said, "It's time now that we think that you will be able to walk on your own, but you will have to make sure that you don't hurt yourself again, all right?"

I replied, "Well, I will do my best, although I cannot give you any guarantees whatsoever, okay?"

A short time later, after I was out of hospital, I was still trying my best to get up and move around, and then I started walking around again, although it did take me a good amount of time. It wasn't long before I had another fit, during which I fell down in the living room. I happened to land on my bad leg, and I had been told that if I fell on one of my ankles or either of my legs, it would make my injuries much worse than they had been last time, so it was then to hospital for me. This time the doctor took a great deal of time looking me over, and then he said, "I am very sorry to tell you this, but we think that because of all the injuries you have received in the past, the best thing to do is to give you another operation. However, after this one, you will have to have operations on both legs from just under the kneecap right down to the ankle. What do you think about that?"

I replied, "I have no problem with this, because it seems that it has to be done."

The doctor replied, "Once again we will send you straight up and you will be first on the list."

I was sent upstairs to the operating room and then taken into the ops ward. After the operation, which I was told lasted four and a half hours, I very slowly started to wake up, and soon I had a good look at my leg. The doctor told me it would never be able to come off and that this was the best it was going to get. Thinking about all this, I said to the doctor, "Is this going to be on for the rest of my life?"

The doctor replied, "I am very sorry, but it will. It will never be able to change."

CHAPTER 11

THE COMPLAINTS

AT THIS POINT, WE WERE having quite a lot of trouble with the hospital. The complaints officer said, "I am very sorry to tell you this, but we are not allowed to tell you over the phone without your son's permission."

My mum replied, "Well, he is right here if you would like to talk to him."

He said, "I am very sorry to say this, but we have sent you two separate letters. Both of them are same, but we need two different signatures, if that is all right with you. You should be receiving them within the next couple of days."

My mum said, "Okay then, thanks," and then she put the phone down. It was then that she told me about what was said, including about the letters.

We waited only a day and a half, and then the letters arrived, one addressed to me and the other to my mum. I started reading mine, which said, "We would require both signatures, from yourself and also your daughter."

Well, as you might imagine, I thought this was hilarious, for the reason that I don't ever remember being given the favour of receiving it. Now, don't put me down. I have put it around on a regular basis, and none of the ladies have ever complained yet, but I don't have either a daughter or a son—unless I was just a little bit drunk one time and was forced into having to make love to some lovely young lady. But if this is a fact, I don't remember it.

My mum's letter was also odd. It said that the hospital required two signatures, my brother's and my sister's. Now, there are a good couple of problems with this, namely, with me being the baby of the family, one of my brothers and his wife live down by Stevenage, and I really don't get one with them at all (I don't know why, but I do know that it was my fault). My sister lives right here just around the corner from us and would do anything for our mum, but once again, we don't get along with each other either (I do know that this one is definitely my fault). Then I have a best mate of a brother, called Barry. We have always been best friends; however, Barry and his beautiful wife Dee live over in Ireland.

Well, the two of them turned up on the doorstep, and I almost fell on the floor in shock, as they were going to spend the next two nights with us, which was great. They placed their bags in the front living room, and we all had something to eat, and then we walked out into the backyard and started laughing and drinking. Then it happened: I collapsed to the ground. Now, I do know that both of them are first-aid trained, so my mum dropped down to the floor, and of course once again I was dripping in blood, so she ran into the house to get one of the first-aid kits. When she came back outside, there was Barry using his body to shield my body from the sun. If either one of us needed help for anything, it would only take a phone call, and then everything would stop, and it would be dealt with as quickly as possible.

After the both of us read each other's letters, my mum got on the phone and said to the complaints officer, "I was hoping you might be able to help me out with the two letters that we have just received this morning."

The officer replied, "Well, yes, I hope you are pleased with them."

At this point, my mum just laughed and then placed her head in her hand, and I thought, *Oh no, here it comes.* She said, "You are having a laugh at me are you not?"

"No, not by any means. Is it not what you were hoping for?"

"Well, let me just read you both these letters, and then I will tell you about all the mistakes, if that is all right with you."

After my mum told him all the mistakes contained in the letters, he came back with, "Well, I am very sorry to hear about this. However, in a hospital of this size, there are bound to be a few typing mistakes at times."

To this my mum replied, "You have got to be joking, and even if you are, is this the right way to do your job? We have not been told about anything. Also, what is going to happen about all of this now? So far, everything you have told us never happened. I would like to step up to the top of the pressure plate by telling you that we now have all the pictures of my son's injuries, and also I have now photocopied all the letters that I have received from you, and as of today, I am going to send all this information to both our solicitor and to our local newspaper. So you can make your own mind up: either brush this incident under the carpet or get on with your job—and I do mean at a much faster and better level than you have so far. I will be hoping to hear from you directly. Thank you for your time and goodbye."

CHAPTER 12

THE REPLY

MY MUM PUT THE PHONE down, and the two of us had a good laugh about it all. Mum said to me, "Well, do you think he will get the point of that?"

A day after my mum told him about our plans, he got back in touch with us. "I have asked three of my team members to have a good look into each and every one of these issues, and I would like to say that I am very sorry about all this, and we will try our best to resolve it for you." Soon after we heard this, we received another letter from the hospital. This one was like a great big fairy tale; almost nothing made any sense whatsoever. So as you might imagine, my mum was not pleased to read it, so she rang his office and said, "What is going on? We have just received another letter from your office, and once again nothing in this letter makes any sense. I don't know anybody who is only in A&E for one hour. I mean, I have never heard of this happening in my lifetime. Once again, thanks for your time." Again she hung up on him.

A day later, the newspapers got in touch with his department, and things turned around suddenly. He replied to the newspapers, "You are not allowed to ask me about any of my patients. I hope you understand this." He then put the phone down on them and decided to give us a call. "Hello, would you like to come into my office today so we can try and get all the information straightened out for you both?"

My mum is the type of person that speaks her mind very clearly and with conviction, and she will not stand down for anything. She replied, "Well, just what do we have to talk about? You keep saying that everyone in your departments is doing their job to a high standard and that nothing ever goes wrong. Is this not what you are going to tell me again?"

As you might imagine, it didn't take him long to respond. "I really do think that we should talk to each other, don't you?"

"Well, just what topic are we going to be talking about this time, and at the end of the day, will it make any difference. All you seem to be doing is to try and cover up your own mistakes? If you cannot start to give me some helpful information within the next two days, my solicitor is waiting for me to tell her to proceed to take this matter as far and as quickly as possible. I have already sent all your letters and all the photos of my son's injuries to her. So I will give you two days only, and if nothing is done, then I hope you know what the consequences might be to both your department and also the other departments that my son was in, not to mention your hospital in general. I imagine a lot of people who hear about this will not be very happy."

The doctor replied, "Look, I really don't think that we have to take this matter any further, do you?"

My mum was not a bit happy to hear this, as you can imagine. She raised her voice slightly and replied, "*No*. From now you have two days and only two days, and if you cannot understand that, then we will see what everyone else thinks after all this is put on Facebook. I am sure you will enjoy all the questions that you will be asked about it. So all the best and thanks for your time." Once again she put the phone down on him.

CHAPTER 13

THE OUTCOME

WELL, AFTER THE SECOND DAY, we still hadn't received any information about the matter, so my mum rang up to speak to her solicitor. "I now have no choice. I do believe that the only course of action left for us is for yourself to take over the case from your end, if that's all right for you."

The solicitor replied, "I have no problem with serving your needs, and yes, I will take on the case. Our team will be gathering together all the documents and as much information as possible. I myself will be talking to you on a regular basis and also having a good talk about just what is going on. I hope that this will satisfy your interests."

My mum replied, "Thank you for your support on this matter."

The solicitor then got straight onto the chief complaints officer. "Why, hello there, I am the solicitor for the Hogarth family, and as of tomorrow, you will not be able to make any contact with the family. The only person that you will be able to speak to is myself. I want this to be clearly understood. I have been given full power to act on the family's behalf and to ask you for any and all medical records and case reports. I would like all this sent to my office as soon as possible. I will also be sending you a letter tomorrow morning, and you will have to sign the document to say that you have received it and then sign it again to say that you have understood all the information contained within the letter. After you have signed both letters, you will be left with one, and the other one will be signed for by you and sent back to our office. Thanks for your time and goodbye."

Just as she promised, the very next day, the letters arrived at the complaints department desk. The man who had brought them said to the secretary, "Hi, there. I am looking for the complaints officer."

She got onto her boss and said to him, "The man you were expecting has just arrived, sir."

He replied, "Will you please send him in."

The man walked into the office and the officer said, "Hi, there. My name is Bill."

The other man said, "Oh, how funny. My name is Ben. We must be flowerpot men. All right then, Bill, I hope that you are ready to start this: I need you to sign this form and I will sign it too. This is just to say that you have received this letter. Then I would like you to read this one and sign to say that you have received it and read it and understood the contents. I will then also sign it as well. And the last one is to tell you that you now have a court order against you to strictly prohibit you from making any contact with the family whatsoever from this point on. Is all of this fully understood, Bill?"

He replied, "Yes, no problem."

After both of them had finished filling in the forms, Ben said, "Could you please do me a favour and give me a photocopy of them all to take back to my office?"

Bill picked up his phone and said, "Will you come into my office?"

His secretary walked into the room and said, "Is there anything I can do for you?"

He picked up all the letters and said, "Yes, will you have these letters photocopied for me please."

"Yes, I will be right back with them."

Bill then said, "Would you like to sit down for a minute while she's doing the letters?" and so the two of them sat down and neither of them spoke.

His secretary walked back into the office a couple of minutes later and placed both letters on the table. Ben said, "Thank you very much." The two men shook hands and then Ben turned around and walked out of the office.

CHAPTER 14

THE COURT DATE

IT HAD BEEN A LONG while since the hospital got in touch with our solicitor, and he said that his team were going to look through all my medical records from all the departments I had been in and see if they could spot any mistakes in any of the treatment I had received. However, because they didn't send anything else to my solicitor after they were served with the original paperwork, me and my mum found ourselves sitting in the courtroom with a great deal of paperwork out on the desktop.

At this point, the judge walked into the courtroom. Someone said the judge's name and then, "Will you all please rise," and when the judge had sat down, he said, "You may be seated." He then went over to the jury members and asked each of them, "Will you please place your hand on the Bible and swear to listen to all of the information contained within this court case." As the Bible was placed in front of each of the jury members, they agreed to the terms. Then they were asked to sit down, and then the case got underway.

The judge looked over at our solicitor and said to her, "All right then, would you like to start us off?"

She started by telling the court all about my fits and injuries on that particular afternoon. When she said this, the solicitor representing the hospital stood up and said, "Objection. There is no proof that the defendant was having so many fits on that afternoon."

My solicitor replied, "Well, yes there is. I have a recording of the 999 officer that day. She was listening to each of my client's fits and asked my mum to tell her each time I had a fit. She is here to talk to the court about the incident."

The judge replied, "I would like to hear the tape of the incident first, please."

The tape was played for him, and all the jury members were taking notes. Next the officer for the court asked the woman from the emergency department to step up to the witness box, and our solicitor asked her, "Is this yourself speaking on this tape?" The emergency department lady replied, "Yes, it is me. I would also like to say that I have been given a report from my department that requires me to place my identity card in the computer and then key in my password, so there can be no question of it being anyone but me who answered this phone call."

The court officer replied, "Thank you very much. You can now take your seat."

After all of this had been said before the court, we had another two witnesses: the ambulance men on that day. The court officer got up from his chair and asked one of the drivers to step into the witness box, and then the court officer said, "Can you please describe what the gentleman looked like at the moment of your arrival at his house for the court, please."

"Well, he was lying on the floor, and he was covered in blood. I tried to see where about the blood was coming from, and I noticed that there were a few cuts on his face, so I cleaned them up and placed some strips on to stop the bleeding. Next, I noticed that he had bitten into the top left-hand side of his lip. There was not much else I could do for him, so I placed a single strip on his lip, and then I took his blood pressure, which was a little bit higher than normal, so I decided to place a line in his vein to try and slow down his blood pressure until we got to the hospital. However, a large amount of his veins had collapsed because of the amount of blood that he had lost; it took me four attempts before I could get the line into place. Then we all arrived at the hospital. It was very busy, and we were waiting for I would say two and a half hours at least before we were able to get logged in and hand over our service sheet to the staff members." After this statement, the ambulance man was asked to leave the witness box.

Now that this had been reported to the court, our solicitor started to read out documents, and it didn't take long before the other solicitor said, "Objection. I would like to see a copy of those papers please." So my solicitor walked over to the court officer and showed him the two letters, and the court officer gave a copy to a different person, and then the court officer turned around and showed it to the judge, and the judge said, "Please will you show this document to the members of the jury."

They were given all the documents to look at, and they were all placed into evidence. Then the judge said to the hospital solicitor, "Could you please tell me why it is that you want to see documents which you know that your company and your clients have already signed for and which you must have in your case folder. There are three different letters here, and each and every one has your signature on it. They are the same as the letters that the complaints have. Can you explain this for me, please?"

The other solicitor then replied, "Yes, Your Honour. You see, my client was pressured into signing these documents, as he was threatened by the other family members that all the information about this case would be placed on Facebook. They also told my client that they would get in touch with the newspaper, which they did, because my client has been contacted by a local newspaper. However, the newspapers were unable to use any of this information, as it is strictly prohibited to give or talk to anyone about someone else's medical records."

The judge looked over to our solicitor and said, "Is any of this true?"

"Yes, Your Honour. The family were not getting any information back from the complaints department, and also all the letters they had previously received were full of spelling errors.

The complaints team then replied, "Well, in a hospital of this size, sometimes spelling errors creep in. But at the end of the day it is not a case of national security."

The judge then replied to the complaints department, "Are you sure you want to have all this information marked as evidence?"

"Yes, Your Honour, this is exactly what my client would like to have done."

The judge then said to the court officer, "Would you like to place these papers in the evidence pile of hospital documentation?" The court officer then placed them in the hospital box pile, and obviously my family and myself had a documentation box as well.

The court officer then said to our solicitor, "Would you like to continue?"

Our solicitor replied, "Well, after hearing from the emergency phone call controller and also from the ambulance service, are you still going to try and tell us that my client has been given the best level of medical care, because from what I have heard, there were a few mistakes. There is a large amount of evidence from both people, as well as the lack of medical communication from the hospital to the family."

The judge then asked, "Have you finished for now?"

"Yes, thank you, Your Honour. May I have all these records marked into evidence please?"

"So noted," replied the judge, and then he said to the court officer, "Will you please confirm these documents for the court please." The court officer placed them in our evidence box, and we were told that the court would now be closing for dinner time and that there would be two armed officers standing next to both the evidence boxes, as well as two guards outside the courtroom.

We all went out for something to eat, and we had guards walking around in between us all just to make sure that there was no trouble. After we had all finished our dinner, we went back into the courtroom, and it was time for the hospital's solicitor to make the arrangements for the hospital. The court officer said, "If you would like to proceed with your defence for the court."

With this, the solicitor stood up and said to us all, "Your Honour, ladies and gentlemen of the jury, you have heard one side of this case, and now we are here to give you a summation of the details, which are as follows. You have heard statements from the emergency dispatcher and also from the ambulance service. Then there are the medical records that we looked into regarding the case for the family after we first heard their complaint about their experience with our teams. As you see, Mr Hogarth was waiting in A&E for only thirty minutes, and then he was released from the hospital."

At this point, our solicitor stood up and said, "Objection, Your Honour, if I may." The judge nodded slightly at her, and she went on, "Well, I have never in my life heard of anyone who has been in A&E being released within thirty minutes. The fact is that Mr Hogarth was sent up for an X-ray and was then admitted to a ward for five days. He was still walking around when going to the toilet and for a shower. Then, after the five days that he was in the ward, he was discharged from the hospital, and then after two days he received a phone call from a doctor, who said to come back into the hospital as soon as possible, because he had looked over the X-rays again, as he was under the impression that there was a strong possibility that my client's leg was fractured. So the family went back in, and after a long wait they were called for, and the doctor confirmed that it was definitely fractured. It was then that my client asked if he was going to get another X-ray, to which the doctor said, 'Oh no, we will just use the first one.' They placed a plaster on his leg, and after it had dried he was allowed to leave. He was told that he should come back in a week, but when they rang up the hospital, the fracture clinic said that they didn't have any record of Mr Hogarth. He then said that he would ring the complaints department, and the receptionist said that she had arranged an appointment for of two o'clock. So they were taken in to see the doctor, and after the plaster was taken off, he said that it was still damaged and the swelling had started to get worse. With this news, the doctor gave my client a boot to wear for at least two weeks. Thank you for your time, Your Honour."

The judge looked up at the hospital's solicitor and said, "Is there any record in your papers that relates to any of this?"

The solicitor said, "Yes, Your Honour, we do have records to support this."

The judge replied, "Why were none of these documents mentioned in the first session?"

The hospital solicitor replied, "We are very sorry, Your Honour, but these papers have only just been found in the back of our records."

The judge replied, "Well, I hope you know that I don't believe this story. However, I don't have to make any decisions on this matter, so I will now ask the jury to step out of the courtroom to decide the outcome of this case. We will be back in court in two hours for the verdict. Thank you all for your time."

Everyone rose and went out to have something to eat. Once again there were guards between both parties, and we were looking at them while we discussed what might happen with the case. We were all called back into the courtroom, and when we went in and sat down, the jury was already there.

The court officer said, "Please rise," and then the judge sat himself down and the court officer said, "Please be seated."

The judge asked the head of the jury to stand up and said, "Can we have your findings, please?"

"Your Honour, we are all together apart from one of us, so that is 13-1. We decide in favour of the Hogarth family, given what we have heard of all the hospital's mistakes and what the family have been through. It is with this in mind that we have come to decide what the costs will be that the hospital will have to give to the family for failings in their medical treatment. We have arrived at the amount of £5,000 for lack of medical attention from the A&E department, £5,000 for the lack of attention from the fracture clinic, and then another £10,000 for the lack of attention from the chief of the complaints department. We all agree on this, Your Honour."

The judge banged his gavel and the court officer said, "Will you all stand, please." The judge summed up by saying, "This decision is final, and this case is now concluded. Thank you all for your time."

As the hospital's representatives were walking past us, they all looked at us, seemingly unhappy with the outcome of the case. We, however, were over the moon and were already planning where to go on our next holiday. We still have not decided, but having won the case, we are sure that we will get there soon, wherever it may be.

Printed in the United States
By Bookmasters